I Spy Books for All Ages:
I SPY: A BOOK OF PICTURE RIDDLES
I SPY CHRISTMAS
I SPY EXTREME CHALLENGER!
I SPY FANTASY
I SPY FUN HOUSE
I SPY GOLD CHALLENGER!
I SPY MYSTERY
I SPY SCHOOL DAYS
I SPY SPOOKY NIGHT
I SPY SUPER CHALLENGER!
I SPY TREASURE HUNT
I SPY ULTIMATE CHALLENGER!
I SPY YEAR-ROUND CHALLENGER!

Books for New Readers:
SCHOLASTIC READER LVL 1: I SPY A BALLOON
SCHOLASTIC READER LVL 1: I SPY A BUTTERFLY
SCHOLASTIC READER LVL 1: I SPY A CANDY CANE
SCHOLASTIC READER LVL 1: I SPY A DINOSAUR'S EYE
SCHOLASTIC READER LVL 1: I SPY A PENGUIN
SCHOLASTIC READER LVL 1: I SPY A PUMPKIN
SCHOLASTIC READER LVL 1: I SPY A SCARY MONSTER
SCHOLASTIC READER LVL 1: I SPY A SCHOOL BUS
SCHOLASTIC READER LVL 1: I SPY FUNNY TEETH
SCHOLASTIC READER LVL 1: I SPY LIGHTNING IN THE SKY
SCHOLASTIC READER LVL 1: I SPY SANTA CLAUS

And for the Youngest Child:
I SPY LITTLE ANIMALS
I SPY LITTLE BOOK
I SPY LITTLE BUNNIES
I SPY LITTLE CHRISTMAS
I SPY LITTLE LEARNING BOX
I SPY LITTLE LETTERS
I SPY LITTLE NUMBERS
I SPY LITTLE WHEELS

Also Available:
I SPY CHALLENGER FOR GAME BOY ADVANCE
I SPY JUNIOR: PUPPET PLAYHOUSE CD-ROM
I SPY JUNIOR CD-ROM
I SPY SCHOOL DAYS CD-ROM
I SPY SPOOKY MANSION CD-ROM
I SPY TREASURE HUNT CD-ROM

# I SPY

## A BOOK OF PICTURE RIDDLES

Photographs by Walter Wick

Riddles by Jean Marzollo

SCHOLASTIC INC.

New York   Toronto   London   Auckland   Sydney
Mexico City   New Delhi   Hong Kong   Buenos Aires

For Linda

W.W.

Book design by Carol Devine Carson

Go to www.scholastic.com for website information
on Scholastic authors and illustrators.

Wick, Walter.
    I spy: a book of picture riddles / photographs by Walter Wick;
riddles by Jean Marzollo; designed by Carol Devine Carson.
        p.   cm.
    "Cartwheel Books"
        Summary: Rhyming verses ask readers to find objects in the
photographs.
        ISBN 0-590-45087-5
        1. Picture puzzles — Juvenile literature.   [1. Picture Puzzles.]
I. Marzollo, Jean.   II. Title.
GV1507.P47W52   1992
793.72—dc20                                                        91-28268
                                                                      CIP
                                                                      AC

Reinforced Library Edition
ISBN-13: 978-0-439-68419-4
ISBN-10: 0-439-68419-6

12  11  10  9  8                                        16 15 14 13/0

Printed in Malaysia         108
This edition, March 2005

# TABLE OF CONTENTS

Picture riddles fill this book;
Turn the pages! Take a look!

Use your mind, use your eye;
Read the riddles and play I SPY!

I spy a rabbit, eleven bears in all,
A dog on a block, a seal on a ball;

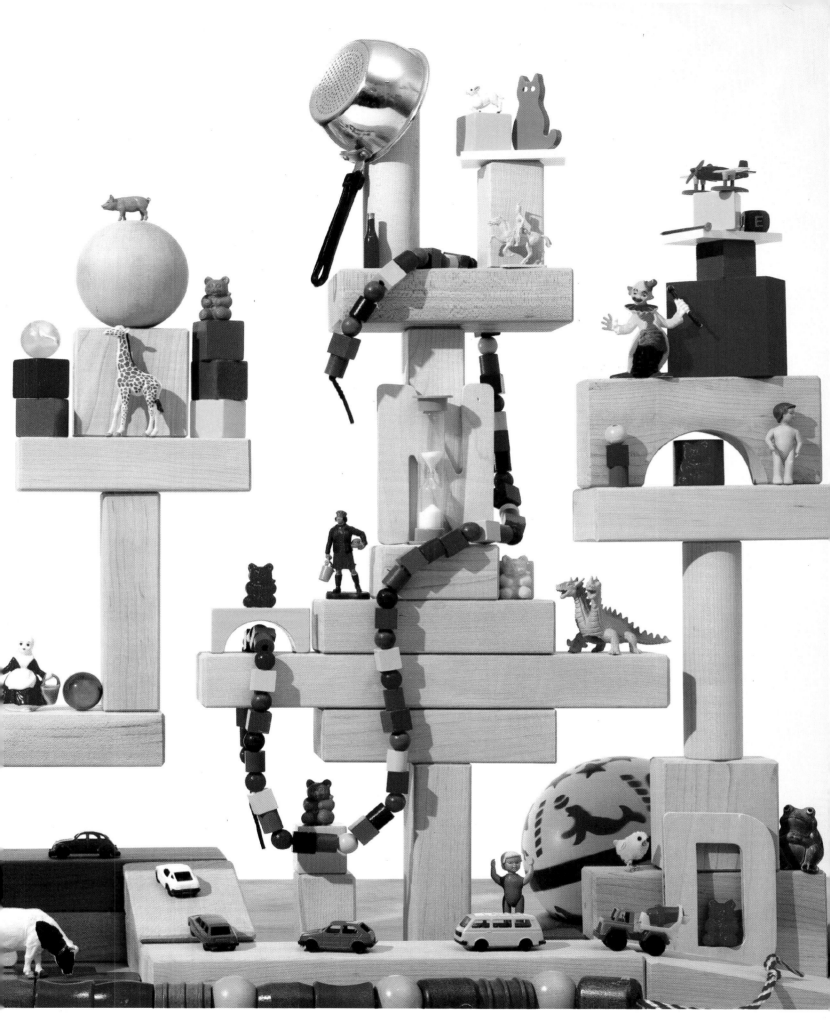

One red bottle, one rubber band,
A wooden craftstick, and the letters in HAND.

I spy a lion and eight other cats,
  A shell from the ocean, a fish who wears hats;

A horse that rocks and a horse that rolls,
A button with a square and one without holes.

I spy a shovel, a long silver chain,
A little toy horse, a track for a train;

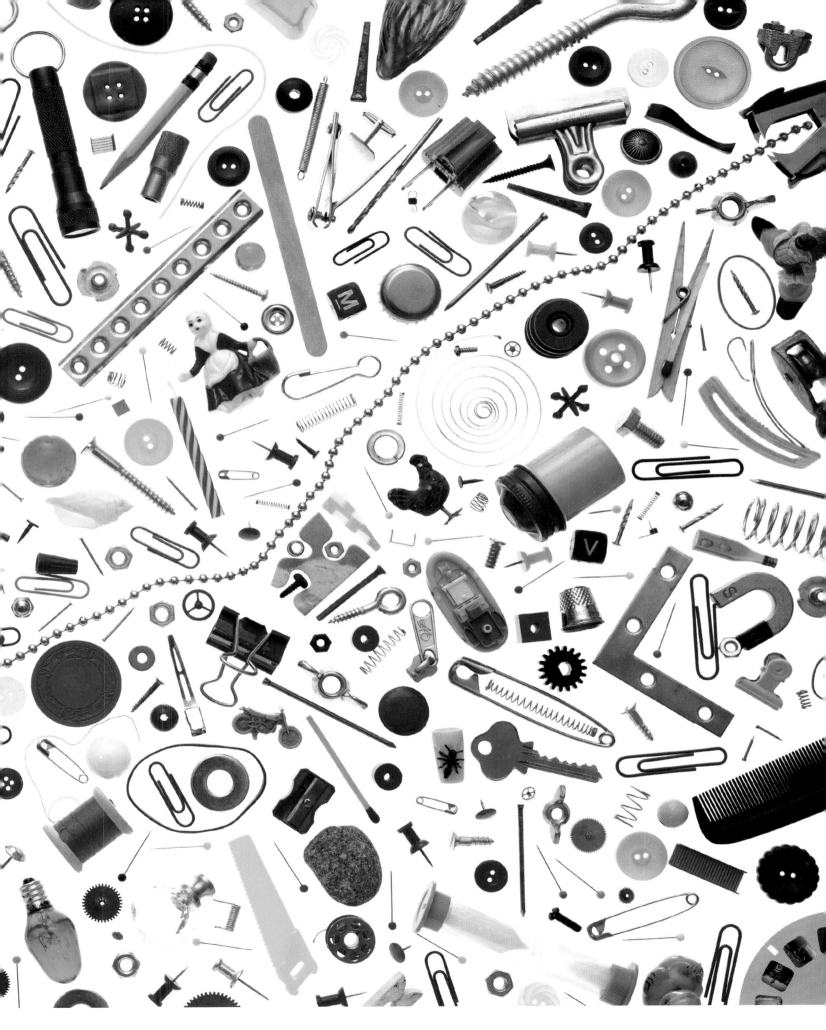

A birthday candle, a pretty gold ring,
A small puzzle piece, and a crown for a king.

I spy a starfish, the feather of a bird,
Thirty-one cents, and a very SANDY word;

A little baby's footprint, a rattle with bells,
A crab, a fork, and seven seashells.

I spy a snake, a three-letter word,
And flying underneath, a great white bird;

Nine gold stars, a blue tube of glitter,
One clay cat, and a six-legged critter.

I spy a stamp, a boy with a plane,
A key on a ring, a song about rain;

Two striped socks, a spaghetti-sauce face,
A girl on a swing, and a snowcapped place.

19

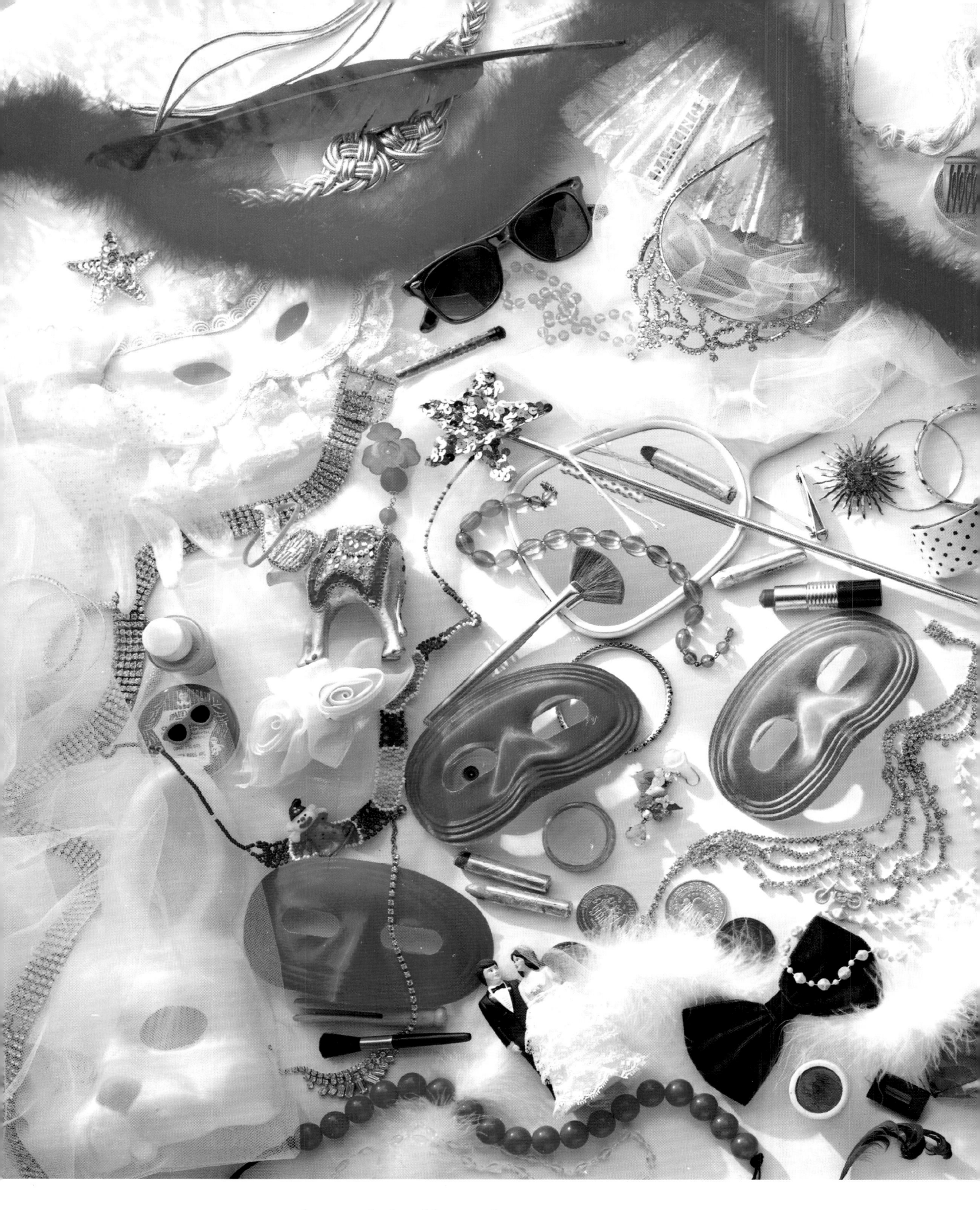

I spy a wand and ballet slippers,

A bird on a scarf, and fingernail clippers;

A bunny-rabbit mask, a heart-shaped box,
A birthday candle, and a key that locks.

I spy an arrowhead, a little white goose,
A horse's shadow, a snake on the loose;

One egg that's white, another that's blue,
A tiger in the grass, and a small turtle, too.

I spy a lamb, a small silver jack,
A bright yellow pencil, a blue thumbtack;

Two black arrows, a red ladybug,
A little puppy dog, and an Oriental rug.

I spy a clothespin, one silver dime,
A little round face that used to tell time;

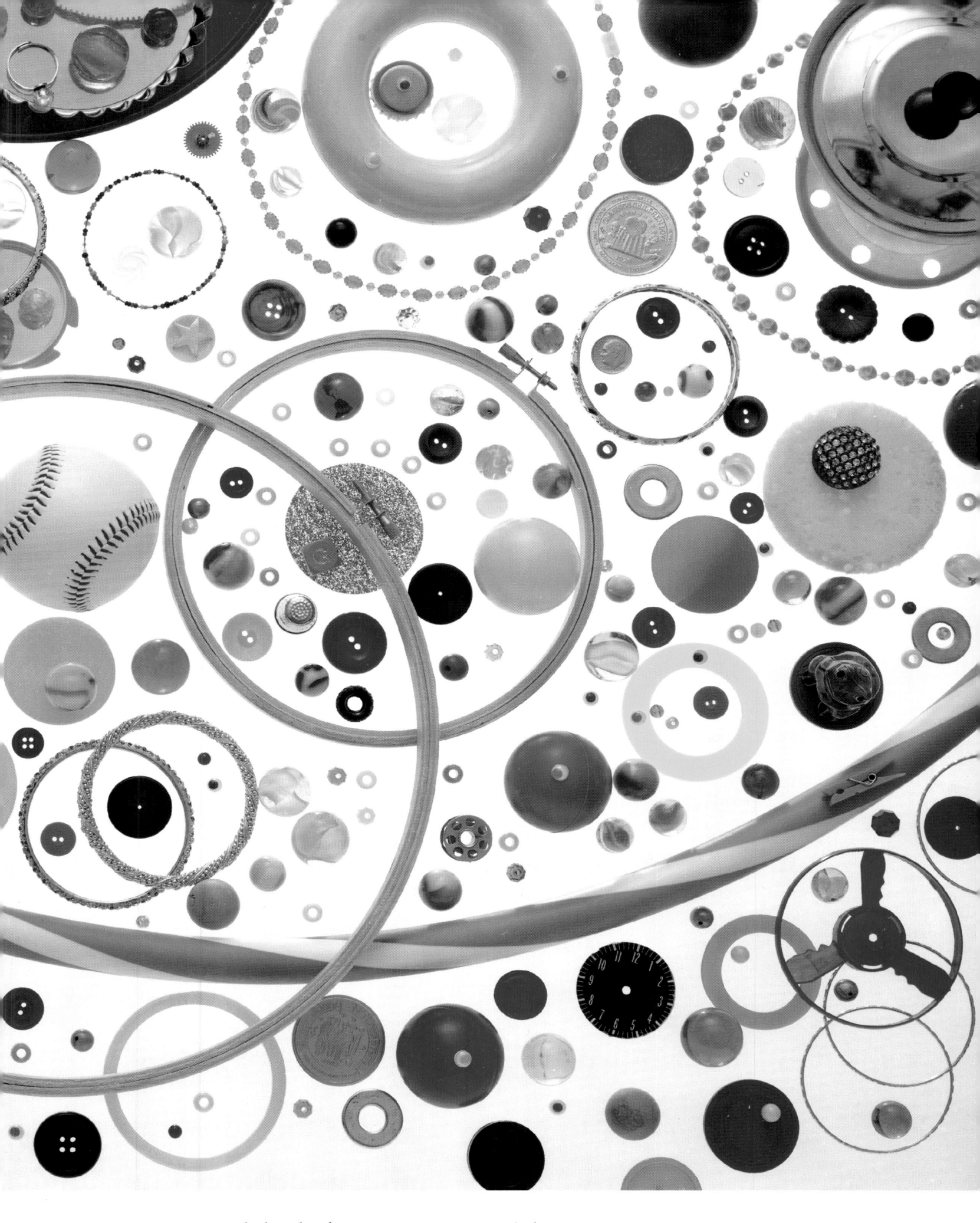

One red ladybug, one gold star;
A new baseball, and a wheel for a car.

I spy a squirt gun, a cowboy hat,
Six airplanes, and a baseball bat;

The point of a pencil, a whistle with a star,
Two yoyos, and a screw near a car.

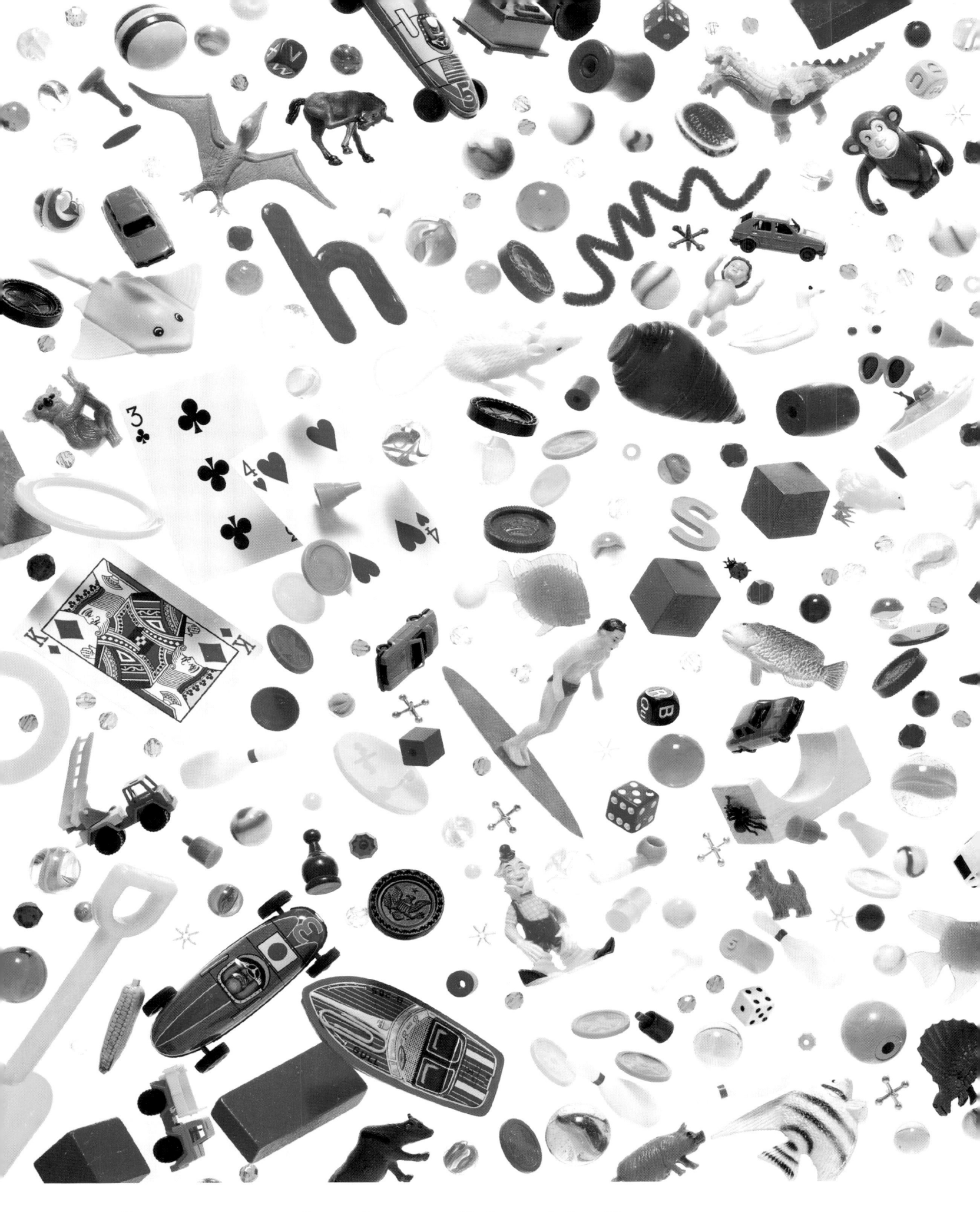

I spy an eagle, eleven fish with fins,

A yellow paper clip, and ten bowling pins;

A bright red phone, a pink baby shoe,
A spider that's black, and an eight that's blue.

I spy an anchor, a musical note,
A crayon and a snake and a small billy goat;

A pair of sunglasses, a tiny bird cage—
I also spy something from every other page.

# EXTRA CREDIT RIDDLES

## "Find Me" Riddle

I'm little and green; I live in a bog;

I'm in every picture; I am a

## Find the Pictures That Go with These Riddles:

I spy six matches, an electric plug,

A double-decker cone, and a little black bug.

I spy a squirrel, a small blue pail,

A penny in a boat, and one little nail.

I spy three hearts, a bat and a ball,

One king's crown, and five 5's in all.

I spy a jar, a small striped stone,

An old flowerpot, and antlers of bone.

I spy a butterfly, a little pearl ring,

One king's crown, and a toy with a string.

I spy a fish and a small cutting tool,
A craftstick doll, and thread on a spool.

I spy a swan, two silly clowns,
An Indian chief, and two gold crowns.

I spy a blimp, an American flag,
A silver safety pin, and a small price tag.

I spy a sea horse, a lonely flip-flop,
A little fisherman, and a buried bottle top.

I spy a reindeer, a colorful parrot,
A thimble with a plant, and a little orange carrot.

I spy a fish hook nearby a hen,
An elephant, egg, and a ballpoint pen.

I spy a clown and a pretty white glove,
A small white horse, and a couple in love.

I spy a globe, an upside-down heart,
Three sports trophies, and a little red cart.

# I Spy Birthday Riddle
# in the Round

You'll need to give a careful look
All around this birthday book
To solve ten challenges—one per year;
When you're finished, give a cheer.

## Happy 10th Birthday to I Spy!

I spy a double-decker cone on the wall, something reflecting a colorful ball, a carefully handstitched black-eyed sun, and a store where you can PLAY CUCKOO FOR FUN. I spy three little blue butterflies, a smile on an apple with googly eyes, six metal staples all in a row, and a spool on a clever machine that can sew. I spy two clocks that read ten of two, and I spy an EXPERT button for you!

## CONGRATULATIONS!

# Write Your Own Picture Riddles

There are many more hidden objects and many more possibilities for riddles in this book. Write some rhyming picture riddles yourself, and try them out with friends.

## About the Creators of I Spy

**Jean Marzollo** has written many award-winning children's books, including eleven I Spy books and seven I Spy Little books. She has also written: *I Love You: A Rebus Poem; Ten Cats Have Hats; I Am Water; I Am a Star; In 1492; Happy Birthday, Martin Luther King; Shanna's Princess Show; Shanna's Doctor Show; Pretend You're a Cat; Close Your Eyes; Soccer Sam; How Kids Grow; Thanksgiving Cats; Home Sweet Home; Sun Song; Mama Mama; Papa Papa;* and *Do You Know New?* With her grown sons she has co-authored *Football Friends, Hockey Hero, Basketball Buddies,* and *Baseball Brothers.* For nineteen years, Jean Marzollo and Carol Devine Carson produced Scholastic's kindergarten magazine, *Let's Find Out.* Ms. Marzollo holds a master's degree from the Harvard Graduate School of Education. She is the 2000 recipient of the Rip Van Winkle Award presented by the School Library Media Specialists of Southeastern New York. She lives with her husband, Claudio, in Cold Spring, New York.

**Walter Wick** is the photographer of the I Spy books. He is author and photographer of *A Drop of Water: A Book of Science and Wonder,* which won the Boston Globe/Horn Book Award for Nonfiction, was named a Notable Children's Book by the American Library Association, and was selected as an Orbis Pictus Honor Book. *Walter Wick's Optical Tricks,* a book of photographic illusions, was named a Best Illustrated Children's Book by *The New York Times Book Review,* was recognized as a Notable Children's Book by the American Library Association, and received many awards, including a Platinum Award from the Oppenheim Toy Portfolio, a Young Readers Award from *Scientific American,* a *Bulletin* Blue Ribbon, and a Parents' Choice Silver Honor. Mr. Wick has invented photographic games for *Games* magazine and photographed covers for books and magazines, including *Newsweek, Discover,* and *Psychology Today.* A graduate of Paier College of Art, Mr. Wick lives with his wife, Linda, in New York and Connecticut.